Conte

CW01500384

Training children's concentration - Practical guide with simple exercises

Attention deficit, mindfulness for children, highly sensitive children, self-esteem

By

Martin J. Stowing

Introduction

Lack of concentration is a problem that affects the lives of a great many parents and children nowadays. It manifests itself in various areas of daily life, for example in difficulties finishing homework for school, distractions appearing during small activities or not listening to what is being said.

Nevertheless, it is crucial to understand that the attention deficit is not a defect but on the contrary, if properly channeled, can become a strength. For this to happen, it is essential to know what causes poor concentration, possible signs, and, most importantly, what strategies can be put into practice to help young children in improving their attention in everyday activities.

This book was created precisely for the purpose of providing all parents with the information and tools they need to help their children in increasing their concentration regardless of their age, whether they are in kindergarten, elementary school, or middle school.

To begin with, we will understand what concentration is and what are the different declinations of attention deficit. Then we will delve from a practical point of view into what elements can affect the attention levels of young children and what techniques, tips and activities we can develop to support children as they grow.

It should be emphasized that this book is not intended as a medical manual since any diagnosis or specific examinations should be carried out by competent figures who can assess the situation and problems found in the child.

This is a simple, practical book that focuses on fun and useful activities for young children. It is dedicated to all parents who wish to help their children in growing up more peacefully, improving their concentration and guiding them to discover their potential.

Chapter 1
What is concentration?

What is meant by concentration

Generally speaking, concentration is understood as the ability to maintain attention on a given task or activity for a reasonable amount of time. This is a fundamental skill, especially in the growing-up period. Concentration, in fact, makes it possible to build positive social relationships and have formative experiences that are important for a child's development.

Although it is considered by many as a single activity or skill, in reality concentration should be considered as a process by which a subject is able to take in and process information. For this process to occur properly, certain elements must be present, namely:

✴ Being able to listen,

✴ Ability to notice verbal and nonverbal signals,

✴ Being able to ignore visual and/or auditory distractions,

✴ Maintain silence when necessary,

✴ Completing tasks and activities,

✳ Recognizing key information.

Looking at concentration from this perspective, it is easier to understand how complex this skill is especially for young children. It requires a lot of effort and a great deal of self-control, which is often still developing in children.

In many cases, poor concentration is associated with a lively attitude that leads the child to become distracted or to fail to control one or more of the fundamental elements of the process. In other cases, however, the attention deficit is related to a neurological disorder called ADHD, or attention deficit hyperactivity disorder. In these cases, it is important to contact doctors and specialized figures who can make an accurate diagnosis and can help the child overcome the difficulties he or she is experiencing in concentrating and maintaining attention.

The development of concentration in toddlers
Concentration is a process without which new things cannot be learned. For this reason it is a skill

of primary importance especially during the growing and developmental years.

To better understand the roots and mental processes in which it is contained, it is necessary to take a step back and analyze what are the basic steps of learning. The latter, in fact, is structured in three stages:

1.   Input, which is the reception of information through attention.

2.   Processing, which is the consolidation of information through the use of memory and logic.

3.   Output, that is, release of the processed information to the outside world.

It is now easy to see the extreme importance of attention in the learning process since in its absence or deficiency the necessary steps cannot be initiated.

Attention, in turn, can be divided into five dimensions:

1.   Generalized attention: understood as the potential intensity of a given subject's attention.

2.   Selective attention: refers to the ability to focus on relevant stimuli and ignore irrelevant ones.

3.   Sustained attention: refers to the ability to remain cognitively focused on specific stimuli.

4.   Divided attention: commonly called multitasking, it is the ability to focus on multiple tasks at the same time.

5.   Shifting attention: understood as the ability to alternate one's attention between two tasks that do not have to be done at the same time.

All dimensions of attention find application in different contexts of daily life and for this reason should be equally relevant.

Yet what many people do not know is that children, as they grow, do not increase the volume of information they are able to handle but efficiency. As toddlers grow, they learn to become "better" at performing the cognitive processes necessary to acquire, control, and select the information they are subjected to.

At this point it is easy to see how the focus of concentration is on the proper cognitive development of the child.

For cognitive development to occur, the selective skills of attention must be improved through the proper detection and determination of important information according to the required outcome. Once this is learned, the child's attention will become increasingly flexible and able to shift in relation to goals. At the same time, the ability to inhibit information not relevant to the goal will also develop.

In general, selective attention and focused attention are fully developed around the age of seven, while maintained attention continues to develop until the age of eleven.

Self-regulation, understood as the use of plans, cognitive strategies and behavioral lines, follows the growth of the frontal lobes of the cerebral cortex; for this reason it develops between the ages of three and ten.

Children begin to recognize and reflect on attention around age four, yet it is only around age seven that they are able to understand that distractions are not only due to external factors but also internal ones. It is also during these years that they begin to develop the idea that motivation and engagement are two key elements in increasing their attention.

The importance of concentration in school and in everyday life

As a result of what was said in the previous paragraph, it becomes rather easy to fully understand the fundamental role of concentration in children's growth and daily life. Concentration, in fact, is essential to perform all school and personal activities effectively.

It is a complex skill that on some occasions is difficult to implement even for us adults. How many times have you been distracted or not really focused on what you are doing? If on some occasions it is difficult even for you to be attentive, try to identify with a child who is constantly receiving stimuli from the outside world and who is still learning to decipher and filter the really important information. Concentration is a skill that requires continuous practice so that the components involved can work together to make the attention process efficient.

By helping your child improve his or her ability to concentrate, you will offer him or her the opportunity to live a more peaceful life. First of all, a mind that is able to maintain a good level of attention allows any task to be accomplished more quickly, correctly and effectively since no time is lost in processing misleading thoughts or observing or listening for possible distractions. This ability also carries over into athletic or physical performance. Much research has been completed in support of this thesis, which has shown that concentration is one of the most relevant elements in athletes capable of excellent performance. Let us remember that our mind is an extremely powerful engine, capable of exerting full control over our body. Getting connected with it and our thoughts is a key step in being able to direct our mind to relevant information and stay focused.

Chapter 2

—

Attention Deficit

What is attention deficit

Attention deficit disorder (ADHD) usually is a cognitive disorder that causes a mix of hyperactivity and impulsive behavior. Although it is an issue found most frequently in children, it also affects many adults. Attention deficit disorder is such a prevalent disorder that many believe it is the most common neurodevelopment-related issue among children.

Symptoms can be different and vary in intensity, in many cases they are mild manifestations while in other cases the signs may be more obvious. In most cases, symptoms tend to vary over time and growth, which is why adult individuals usually show milder symptoms than in their childhood. Nevertheless, ADD can also cause problems in older people. For example, an adult with this type of problem might have difficulty being focused at work, school, or when relating to friends or relatives. In some cases this translates into difficulties in finding employment or relationship and marriage problems. For this reason, it is important to identify from an early age any signs that may be attributable to attention deficit; in fact, their presence is not a definitive sentence to a difficult life. It is sufficient to identify the path that is most suitable for the child and that can lead him or her to a greater awareness of self and mind.

To avoid misunderstanding, it should be emphasized that if a child is particularly lively and energetic, it does not mean that he or she suffers from attention deficit. On the contrary, energy in toddlers is a signal that helps us understand that they are healthy from both a physical and mental point of view.

Attention deficit occurs when this energy is misplaced and prevents the child from learning, growing, or doing other activities with his or her peers. From a practical point of view, in most cases this results in difficulty in staying attentive, completing tasks or following instructions. In addition, some children tend to be easily distracted by their thoughts, fail to finish activities as they lose interest rather quickly, or have difficulty organizing themselves in an orderly and precise manner.

Before going on to explore attention deficit, its symptoms and causes, it is worth mentioning again that this book has no medical value but is intended to provide useful information for adults who wish to help young children in improving their concentration or solving attention-related problems. If there is any doubt about the presence of symptoms that can be traced to attention deficit, it is essential to consult a professional who can make an assessment on the child and can guide the family in solving the problem.

Possible causes of attention deficit

Currently, possible causes related to the development of attention deficit have not yet been identified; some believe it is a condition developed in response to a number of different causes. All research to date has not yielded convincing results, which is why several studies on attention deficit are still being conducted. Nevertheless, researchers have highlighted some elements that could influence the occurrence of this disorder in young children.

Genetic component

According to some studies, genetics may have an important impact in the potential development of attention deficit. In fact, in several cases, it has been found that children with siblings with AD are more likely to manifest the same condition. The percentage of possibility highlighted in these studies (Faraone, Larsson - 2019) is around 30%-50% and further increases in case the parents also suffer from attention deficit disorder.

For this reason, it is believed that the mother and/or father may pass on genes related to this type of disorder to their children. Of course, this does not mean that the child of a parent with attention deficit disorder will necessarily have the same diagnosis. Certainly, the odds will be higher but it is not certain that such genes will be passed on to their children.

Brain development

Scientists have found that the brain tends to develop more slowly in children in whom attention deficit has been found. It is not uncommon for the brain in these individuals to reach the same performance as their peers later, which is why in many cases the diagnosis of attention deficit cannot be made until the age of nine or ten.

As anticipated in the previous pages, research on the possible causes of this disorder is not yet conclusive and requires more study and investigation, nevertheless some recent research has shown a possible neurological correlation. They have shown that in individuals with attention deficit disorder some parts of the brain are smaller, while others are larger than average.

In addition, researchers believe that identifying the specific neurological development that causes this condition is important in predicting when it will be normalized by the subject.

Environmental factors

Although environmental factors are not usually considered as real causes of AD, they can be relevant risk factors. Some of these may include certain dietary regimens and preservatives, exposure to cigarette smoke, lead contamination, smoking during pregnancy, or low body weight at birth.

Unfortunately, there are no specific actions that can be put in place to prevent the formation of this disorder. In general, what scientists recommend is to give the child a positive and healthy lifestyle as early as possible so that the development of AD is limited as much as possible. Recommended activities include reading books or talking openly about emotions and feelings.

Although there are no studied and approved strategies, what any adult can do is to pay attention to his or her child's behavior and ask for support if there are suspicious attitudes.

Classification of attention deficit and symptoms

ADHD can be classified into three sub-categories: ADHD with reduced attention, ADHD with impulsivity and hyperactivity, or ADHD combined with inattention and impulsivity and hyperactivity.

Each category shares some symptoms, while others are different and specific to each group.

Recognizing the potential signs in each category is critical to understanding what the child is experiencing in his or her everyday life and supporting him or her in times of need. In addition, since individuals with this condition usually do not respond to traditional educational methods, it may be helpful to implement a tailored discipline plan that can properly direct him or her in the growth and development of his or her personality without limitations. Last but not least, recognizing the signs is essential to seek a possible medical diagnosis and to listen to the opinions of professional figures who specialize in this type of condition.

In the next paragraphs we will look at each of the three groups into which attention deficit can be classified and the symptoms related to them.

ADHD with reduced attention

This category of attention deficit has several symptoms. The main sign is easiest to observe is the ease with which children who fall into this group are able to get distracted from an activity. In many cases, these are individuals who have difficulty organizing a particular task or solving games such as Legos or puzzles. They are often described as dreamy children in that they have a tendency to lose concentration and wander freely with their minds in their thoughts.

A child with this type of condition may have difficulty executing precise directions and at first may give the impression that he or she is not listening to what is being said. It is not uncommon for children in this group to lose objects and confuse shoes and socks, as well as have no interest in doing homework or other chores.

In case you find yourself constantly reminding and repeating to your child that he needs to finish his homework or that he needs to take out the garbage, this may be attention deficit. Another sign may come from teachers, especially when your child tends to repeat the same distracting mistakes in tests or homework. This usually occurs because he has lost interest in the exercise or is in a hurry to finish in order to engage in a new activity that has captured his attention.

ADHD with hyperactivity and impulsivity

This type of attention deficit differs from the one just mentioned because in these cases the child is able to pay attention. He has the ability to stay focused on a task or activity in which he is interested, blocking out any stimuli or distractions that might divert his attention.

Children who fall into this category very often are the chatterboxes of the class or family. They usually have a lot to say and tell about any topic and end up talking fast or interrupting others. For example, in a school situation, the child might talk without asking permission or be the "clown" of the class who goes out of his way to make his classmates laugh and have fun. In some cases, he might be represented by a pupil who answers all the teacher's questions without having permission for the simple reason that he cannot control his impulse.

It is not uncommon for ADHD individuals with hyperactivity and impulsivity to be characterized by constant movement and have difficulty remaining still when asked. These are children who tend to move, change positions and wiggle when they are in class and to be much more active and lively than their peers when it comes time for play. To release their energy, these individuals might engage in many different activities such as running, jumping, climbing, playing soccer or even playful brawling.

Another indicator of this type of disorder is being loud and boisterous with other children, even to the point of disturbing the people around them or making scenes.

Those who fall into this category are unable to control their impulses and tend to act without thinking; this means that they fail to consider the consequences of their actions before putting them into practice.

Of course, all of these symptoms can occur in a more or less pronounced way: if your child tends to talk even when not required or has difficulty waiting his turn during an activity, these could be signs related to lack of control but these are minor circumstances. A more relevant signal might be related to situations where the child puts himself in danger without being aware of it, for example, he might chase the ball down the road without checking for oncoming cars.

In general, this category can become dangerous in situations where the child wants to do something, even when the latter is considered dangerous, and does not consider all the bad things that might happen because he considers himself invincible.

Combined ADHD

This last category is a combination of the previous two groups, namely ADHD with reduced attention and ADHD with hyperactivity and impulsivity. Children who fall into this group show symptoms of both categories.

They are usually children who tend to be disorganized, unfocused, dreamy, with a habit of losing objects, confusing instructions, talking even when not required, and having difficulty waiting their turn. In short, patience is not the strong point of these individuals.

In most cases they are noisy children, extremely active and always looking for something new to do from which they end up getting distracted after a short time. This type of subject tends to wiggle and fidget constantly as staying still is something they are unable to do, at least for long periods of time.

Although this category is the most complex to manage, it is important to remember that every problem is solvable. Children with ADHD combined do not need to be excluded or looked at differently from other peers, they simply need more empathy and understanding of their disorder from the people around them.

Symptoms of attention deficit during growth

In many cases, recognizing the symptoms of attention deficit is easier if they are related to the child's age. In fact, this condition shows different signs depending on the age group: a teenager is unlikely to react with the same excitement as a second-grader to being suggested to go to the playground.

0 to 3 years old

Recognizing attention deficit in children three years old or younger is quite difficult as they are still seeking balance in this age group and therefore tend to get agitated and bored easily.

It is complicated to understand whether a child of this age is switching from one game to another due to lack of concentration or because they are simply discovering the world around them. In general, in this age group it is inadvisable to observe any repetitive behavior or difficulty in staying focused on one game or activity. It is preferable to wait and monitor his growth in later years.

4 to 7 years old

Children in this age group are still quite young and are in a developmental stage where they are still learning their limits and the rules of the supervised environments of home and school.

At this age, the child may find it difficult to follow instructions or may choose to ignore them and do things his or her own way. If affected by attention deficit disorder, he may have difficulty controlling impulses and self-regulating; for example, he may touch or pick up objects he has been told not to touch.

One item to watch for is the level of activity and any tendency to fidget or wander around the classroom when he feels bored. It is not uncommon for children with attention deficit to find it difficult to pay attention or listen to what is being said to them: they have a mind full of thoughts, making it almost impossible to stay focused on any one activity. Finally, another sign is the impulse to speak out of turn.

8 to 13 years old

Within this age group are several symptoms that parents or teachers may notice in the child. One over all is constant restlessness and difficulty in remaining still. This is fidgeting that goes beyond the occasional fidgeting typical of children of this age: at school, for example, he may get up from his chair when he wants to and without asking permission. In many cases, it is possible to see that the child is tireless and bored both at home and at school. In addition, he may find it difficult to concentrate on classwork or even forget to do it.

Also in this age group, the child could be described as distracted or dreamy, always focused in his thoughts and not paying much attention to what is happening in the world around him. Usually children with attention deficit between the ages of 8 and 13 do not think about the results of their actions: they want to do what they want to do and they want to do it immediately. They reflect on what they did only when an adult explains to them what the consequences of their actions were.

Ages 14 to 18

Children in this age group can be understood as young adults. They are teenagers, which is why it can be quite complicated to relate to them, even in cases where they do not have attention deficit disorder.

Nevertheless, children with attention deficit disorder of this age usually do not show all the typical symptoms of younger children. One example is the hyperactive component of this disorder, which tends to ease as the child grows.

The most common element is lack of organization in the adolescent: he or she may have difficulty turning in projects by the deadline and fail to prioritize things properly. This approach leads to handing in checks or assignments that are full of errors, not complete or messy.

In many cases, children with ADD are characterized by reckless behavior that leads them to disregard the consequences of their actions. Unfortunately, as they grow older, this type of behavior may endanger the health and safety of the child. These are individuals who tend to act on their impulses, pursuing their ideas without planning or thinking about what might happen.

In this age group, it is important for parents to be even more vigilant as dangerous circumstances are more frequent.

Given the many signs and symptoms and of attention deficit it is quite easy to get confused or doubtful, especially when it comes to one's own children. Indeed, for many adults, it is complicated to understand when a behavior is within the range of normal and when it may be a sign. In any case, the best solution is to communicate openly with the child, teachers, and siblings to analyze the presence of any behavioral patterns that can be traced to attention deficit.

This analysis can be done by taking notes on a daily basis that will be re-read by the same parents after a few months to determine whether professional support is needed or not.

Chapter 3

—

The role of stress and emotions

The influence of stress on concentration

All of us, unfortunately, are familiar with stress. Every human being is forced to confront it at different times in his or her life.

From a scientific point of view, stress is defined as an altered condition that the human body activates as a result of exposure to external or internal stimuli that the subject is unable to satisfy. This situation generates severe pressures that manifest themselves in the form of discomfort from both psychological and physical perspectives.

In children, this condition leads to changes in some of their behaviors, often through aggressive attitudes, mood swings, and reduced attention. Obviously, it is necessary to contextualize the behaviors that are considered abnormal, observing at what times they are enacted and how long ago the change was noticed.

In general, the most common signs of childhood stress are:

- Apathy or lack of interest in activities,
- Sudden changes in mood,
- Exaggerated reactions, tantrums and heightened susceptibility,
- Variations in food tastes and preferences,
- Performance anxiety in school and sports,
- Recurrent headaches and/or stomachaches,
- Poor attention and concentration.

As can be seen from the list just mentioned, poor attention and concentration are counted among the main symptoms of stress. This state of mind, in fact, can greatly affect the life and mental condition of young children, even more so than in adults. To understand this concept, we need to remember that children, especially up to the age of seven, are still at a stage when cognitive functions are developing and may have more difficulty in implementing effective cognitive processes and responses.

Stress, being a consequence of a situation in which the child feels under pressure, absorbs much of the child's mental energy and prevents him or her from focusing on other activities.

The factors that can generate stress can be many and varied in nature. What needs to be considered is the child's personality as a whole: his attitude, his emotional state, and his ability to respond positively to different circumstances. Shyer and more sensitive children are more likely to succumb to stress, which is why it is essential to reinforce and work on the development of self-esteem.

Emotional development

Understanding the stages of emotional development is important for building the most appropriate environment for the child. This is a complex natural process that can greatly influence the behaviors of young children.

0 to 1 year old

As soon as they are born, babies show their emotions in a strong and lively way even though they are not yet able to understand their emotions. They are able to express negative emotions more easily than positive ones. This is a period of great questioning and discovery in which the child, step by step, begins to understand emotions better.

1 to 2 years old

In this age group, children begin to recognize their emotions more easily, regulate it and keep their impulses under control. It is during these months that they begin to see things from another person's point of view. This ability is more commonly known as empathy, which is the ability to recognize another individual's feelings from their own perspective and without losing their own identity.

Years 2 to 5

This period of life is mostly devoted to the development of social skills. At this age the child should be able to interpret the mood of others and react accordingly.

It is only around age 4 that we get to the beginning of the development of self-control, through the achievement of awareness of what it is and how it works.

Finally, at age 5, children develop conscience, beginning to feel guilty after doing something wrong.

Ages 5 to 7

This age group represents one of the biggest childhood changes from the point of view of emotional development. It is during these years that the child will fully understand how to interpret facial expressions and emotions, and begin to understand what is the way to make new friends.

It represents a period in life when they begin to understand more clearly the world around them and gain the ability to listen and consider other people's points of view. Impulse control and impulsive reactions also develop largely between the ages of 5 and 7.

Ages 7 to 10

In these years the child develops his ability to show empathy toward others, improves his ability to listen to other people's point of view, and begins to understand the consequences of his actions on other people.

10 to 13 years old

This age group represents another important time in children's growth as it is characterized by major changes related to emotional development. At this age children become better at recognizing their own feelings and those of others, they also achieve a deeper understanding of how their actions can affect other people.

Control of emotions also becomes stronger at this stage.

From age 13 onward

At this stage children can be called teens since these are the years of entry into the adolescent period. At this age they will have good emotional control and be able to make correct decisions. This is a delicate period as the developments that will take place during these years will have a huge impact on the kind of adult they will become.

Although children are more independent at this age, it is important for parents to watch them from afar and be ready to help them if needed. This is a complicated task for a parent as they must learn to strike the right balance between offering help and letting their child fend for themselves.

Learning to manage emotions

Very often children characterized by poor attention span have hundreds of thoughts constantly crowding their minds, and this is what prevents them from focusing on a single task or activity. Their constant distraction also does not help them in recognizing their emotions or keeping them under control, so they end up overreacting when a sudden feeling takes hold of them.

If managing emotions is difficult for an adult, it is even more so for a child who is still developing his or her pre-frontal cortex, which is the control center for reason, planning, risk assessment, impulses and emotion regulation.

As we elaborated in Chapter Two, children with attention deficits have slower brain development and, for this reason, are more likely to be guided by their emotions. A valuable contribution to improving the ability to recognize one's feelings, thoughts and gain more control is Mindfulness. This is a practice that has been shown to be particularly effective in developing concentration with intention. It involves practicing to learn how to enter a state of total awareness on both the inner and outer levels. While similar to meditation, Mindfulness is different in that it does not require us to completely clear our minds but rather to be totally present in the moment, observing and noticing everything around us.

Among its many benefits, this practice also allows for the development of acceptance, which is why it is particularly suitable for children with attention deficit disorder. Mindfulness can teach them to accept all of life's events, even those we cannot directly control, and deal with them without becoming overwhelmed by stress. In fact, the only thing we can really control is how we decide to respond to what happens around us. From this perspective, Mindfulness is an excellent tool for learning to work with the thoughts, feelings, and reactions that are triggered by certain events.

Moreover, constant practice has been shown to create and strengthen neural connections related to calmness and concentration. Both of these are essential elements for a child with difficulties in maintaining attention.

Creating a positive environment

One effective way to alleviate symptoms related to attention deficit is to create a positive and well-organized environment. In this regard, modifications to the circumstance environment can be put into practice, that is, changes that enable the child to excel in different areas of his or her life. Below are some useful tips that can help create a positive environment for the child:

✓ Organization and routine planning

Organization and routine are two particularly useful tools for children with ADHD, especially when they find it difficult to get organized.

In these cases, parents can help the child plan the day's activities so that all his or her tasks are completed.

Routines also mean the activities needed during transition times, for example, the morning routine includes all the actions to be done in the morning before going to school such as breakfast, brushing teeth, washing face, getting dressed, preparing the folder, and so on. Other examples may be the routine before going to bed or the homework routine. These are small plans that are very helpful in getting the child to complete his or her activities and gain more self-confidence.

✓ Division of tasks.
Especially when the child is faced with complex tasks and activities, it is possible to break them down into small goals collected in a checklist. This is an effective technique as the child will be able to remember everything he or she needs to do and at what time.
Check-lists are often used within routines to remember all the tasks to be done and their order.

✓ Remove unnecessary sounds.
This advice is especially useful at times when the child needs to engage in an activity that requires special attention such as a reading, exercise, or school lesson. Because the child finds it difficult to concentrate in situations where distractions are present, it is important to remove noises or sounds that might divert his attention from what he is doing.

For example, when the child is doing homework, it is advisable to turn off TV, radio or other devices that might distract him. This also applies when bedtime comes. Another useful recommendation is to keep the child away from windows or keep them closed so that outside noise cannot enter.

√ Insert active breaks.
This advice is especially useful at school or while doing homework. It is important to let the child have active breaks in which he or she can vent his or her energy freely. In fact, it has been observed that the inclusion of 5-10 minutes of breaks can greatly improve the concentration abilities of children with difficulties in this area.

√ Choosing the right activities
This is critical because children with attention deficit may have difficulty performing activities that require sitting or standing still for long periods of time. It is preferable to opt for more active activities that make the child feel comfortable and, as a result, more focused on work. For example, instead

of opting to write a report, you can invite him to make a presentation or build a model.

✓ Consolidate processes.

After implementing all the useful environmental modifications to improve the child's development, it is essential to consolidate the processes identified. They need to be constantly repeated so that the child has time to acquire them and make them automatic. This step is crucial when dealing with children with attention deficit; their distraction requires that activities and concepts be repeated several times before they are fully internalized.

Increasing self-esteem in the child

Attention deficit is often associated with low self-esteem and emotional and physical problems. Each of us, regardless of our condition, has within us the strength needed to achieve our goals. When toddlers feel they are not up to par or not good enough, they are limiting their chances for success and losing interest in activity and the outside world. Two rather effective ways to boost self-esteem in the child are to use positive language and pay close attention. It is important to be connected to the child's needs as this will help the child feel more confident. Empathy and understanding emotional and/or physical difficulties are the main tools in this process.

In addition, it is crucial to focus on strengths and minimize weaknesses; when we focus on problems or negative things, the feelings we get in return are of frustration and stress. In contrast, when we focus on possibilities, the feelings we get back are positive and full of energy.

Another aspect that should not be underestimated is that of mistakes: children must be free to make their own mistakes, only then can they reflect on why, how to improve and gain confidence. What is important is that such mistakes are not judged.

Chapter 4

—

The importance of concentration in school and in everyday life

The role of nutrition

Nutrition can play an important role in the proper development and maintenance of concentration. There are foods and supplements that can provide numerous benefits to brain function and, as a result, reduce some of the symptoms associated with attention deficit such as restlessness or the inability to maintain concentration for prolonged periods of time. Similarly, there are foods that should be avoided as they can slow down or make brain function less efficient.

Generally speaking, one can decide between one of the following three alternatives:

1.   Control the diet as a whole.

Here we start from the assumption that the food taken in has the power to improve or worsen the ability to concentrate. Therefore, it will be necessary to prioritize all useful ingredients to improve brain performance.

2.   Taking supplements.

This alternative focuses on adding supplements, vitamins, or other micronutrients important for mental and physical well-being to the diet. The main purpose of this option is to achieve the daily intake of vitamins and nutrients needed to nourish the body.

3.   Remove discouraged foods.

This last route focuses on removing from the diet all foods or ingredients that could worsen symptoms related to poor concentration.

It is important to note that the advice mentioned in this chapter are guidelines and suggestions observed for individuals suffering from attention deficit disorder and in no way replace medical advice. Should you need to create a food plan for your child, it is advisable to consult a nutritionist who can make an ad hoc assessment and choose the best foods for your child.

The best foods for improving attention

In this section we will look at what foods are generally recommended for children who have difficulty staying focused or show signs of hyperactivity.

✓ Unprocessed and additive-free foods.

The dangerous nature of additives makes them unsuitable for young children, so it is advisable to prefer fresh and unprocessed foods. Additives include artificial sweeteners, preservatives, and dyes, all ingredients found in most packaged products. They also lack relevant nutritional values that can benefit children with concentration difficulties.

✓ Chicken

Tryptophan is an important amino acid that is able to promote protein synthesis in the body and increase serotonin production. The latter is particularly important because it supports sleep and happy emotions, thus helping to control impulses and hostilities.

✓ Eating breakfast

In most cases, children with difficulty concentrating derive several benefits from eating a proper breakfast. This meal has the ability to help the body in regulating blood sugar levels and stabilize hormonal fluctuations. If possible, it is advisable to have about 10-15 grams of protein for breakfast. For example, Greek yogurt can be a great way to start the day.

✓ Wild salmon
Wild salmon is not only rich in vitamin B-6 but also has high dosages of Omega-3. It is essential for the efficient functioning of the brain; in some research, Omega-3 has been shown to improve learning and solve some behavioral problems such as those attributable to attention deficit.
All humans, children and adults, should consume wild salmon at least twice a week.

Foods to avoid
In this section we will delve into the foods and ingredients whose consumption should be limited or avoided because they are capable of

increasing concentration difficulties in young children.

✓ Sugar

It is now well known that sugar is one of the most harmful foods for children. If possible, it is recommended to avoid any kind of refined sugar or foods in which it is contained such as chocolate, sweets, sugary drinks or fruit juices.

✓ Gluten

Some researchers and parents have noticed that children's symptoms tend to worsen as a result of gluten intake. This may indicate an increased sensitivity to the protein found in wheat. In these cases, when possible, it is best to limit consumption of gluten-containing foods such as bread, pasta or pizza. Of course, it is possible to do tests and observe any changes in the child's behavior after eating gluten-containing foods. If there are no particular differences, it is not necessary to reduce or eliminate this food group.

✓ Caffeine

Although some studies have shown that caffeine could be useful in treating some symptoms related to behavioral disorders, it is always best to avoid or limit caffeine consumption. In fact, side effects of this beverage include anxiety and nervousness, emotions that could worsen concentration.

√ Dairy products
Cow's milk contains a substance that could trigger the same reaction as gluten. In these cases, just as mentioned above, it is a good idea to observe any changes in the child's behavior after cow's milk intake to assess whether it is necessary to reduce the intake of this ingredient. It can be replaced with goat's milk as the latter is more easily assimilated by the human body.

√ Dyes
Some children are allergic to the dyes in most packaged products. These ingredients, in addition to being present in most commercial foods, are also present in some soft drinks. Some examples

are: energy drinks, chocolate, cake mixes or candy.

✓ Sodium glutamate

This is an additive that is believed to decrease dopamine levels in the bodies of adults and children. Since dopamine is related to pleasure in the brain, it is essential for children who have difficulty concentrating.

✓ Nitrites

These ingredients are usually found in cured meats, canned foods, and other packaged foods. Excessive consumption of nitrites has been linked to the development of type 1 diabetes, the occurrence of some cancers, and irritable bowel syndrome. Reactions triggered by nitrites include rapid heartbeat, difficulty breathing and agitation. As you can easily guess, these responses of the body only worsen the ability to concentrate.

√ Artificial sweeteners
Artificial sweeteners are bad for health, especially when symptoms associated with attention deficit disorder occur. These ingredients trigger biochemical reactions in the body, which could affect cognitive function and psychological balance.

√ Allergens
If possible, it is good to avoid allergens or other foods that might trigger allergic reactions. Some of the most common allergens include: gluten, soy, milk, peanuts, eggs, and shellfish. You can check with your doctor to see if you are allergic to certain ingredients.

Useful supplements

Some experts believe that children with concentration problems should take vitamin and micronutrient supplements daily, while others believe that a balanced, healthy diet is sufficient. There is currently no scientific evidence to show that taking multivitamin supplements can improve attention and focus. Moreover, if taken in excess, they could be detrimental to the child's overall health.

For this reason, before deciding to supplement a toddler's diet with supplements, it is important to consult a physician who can make a sound judgment. In general, the best way to feel better physically and mentally is to identify which foods are worsening symptoms and work to eliminate them from your diet.

Iron

Currently, there are still several ongoing research studies aimed at demonstrating the effects that low iron levels can have on children. Usually, when we think of an iron deficiency, we imagine people who have blood-related problems. In reality it is a key mineral so its deficiency can change the balance of the entire body, even go as far as increasing symptoms of ADD.

Iron is so important to the human body because, among its various tasks, it has to make sure that oxygen reaches the muscles and vital organs. These include the brain and its proper functioning.

In addition, iron deficiency can slow down the production of dopamine, which, as we saw earlier, is essential for a peaceful and healthy life.

Omega 3

Recent studies have shown that increasing consumption of good fats, such as those found in omega-rich foods, can support and increase dopamine production in the brain.

These types of fatty acids are particularly useful for the proper functioning of brain function and, consequently, for improving concentration and limiting symptoms of attention deficit. Omega-3s also prove effective in reducing restlessness, impulsivity, hyperactivity, and more generally the aggressiveness that can be found in some children. Toddlers can have numerous benefits from proper omega 3 intake, whether through food or supplementation.

A holistic approach to nutrition

It is widely believed that a diet high in sugar, salt, and fat and low in whole grains, fruits, and vegetables can cause various damage to the body. This is also true for children who have difficulty concentrating.

Natural foods and drinks can promote a better state of mind, and a diet based on healthier, tastier alternatives can be a valuable support for proper development.

Here are a number of small tips that can be applied to everyday life:

- Snacks: instead of buying snacks or other packaged products, snacks can consist of fresh fruits and vegetables. Smoothies and shakes are a great alternative, and since they are simple to make, it can be fun to invite children to help you prepare them.

- Clean eating: this advice refers to avoiding, whenever possible, the consumption of foods with unnecessary additives and dyes. It is normal for children to be attracted to colored candies and products rich in chocolate or cream. Yet, as parents, we have a responsibility to buy foods that can support children's health.

- Vitamin D: This vitamin is also called the sunshine vitamin because it is absorbed by the body when we spend time in the sunlight. Unfortunately, nowadays many children spend most of their time indoors; to avoid this deficiency, it is important to make sure that toddlers spend at least 20 minutes outdoors every day. You can organize a walk, a soccer game, a bike ride or a picnic. Vitamin D, in fact, can maintain high levels of serotonin in the body and ensure a good balance.

- Legumes: legumes are a great ingredient to add to toddlers' diets and can be introduced in a fun way, for example by making burritos or hummus. These foods are rich in fiber, which is essential for the health of young and old alike.

- Alternatives to dairy products: some people have difficulty digesting cow's milk products. If your child falls into this category try tasty alternatives that can replace it: such as almond, soy, hazelnut or oat-flavored drinks. In addition, it is helpful to supplement the diet with probiotic foods that can promote gut wellness and, consequently, mood. Some examples are kefir or Greek yogurt.

Chapter 5

—

The motivation

The importance of motivation

Motivation is defined as the engine that drives one to enact a behavior and carry it forward over time to achieve a goal. The stronger this drive, the more likely the subject is to take the action and continue it over a long period of time despite possible obstacles or setbacks.

Given this premise, it is easy to see how motivation and focus are closely related. Motivation, in fact, is a key element that allows one to properly activate concentration and devote oneself to an activity for an extended period of time.

In order for a child to be motivated, however, it is necessary that a need, interest or desire is ignited within him or her that drives him or her to act in a certain way.

This concept is especially true in the school setting since many children's difficulties, including in terms of attention, depend on a lack of motivation and interest in learning or specific subjects.

In this regard, it may be useful to point out the difference between intrinsic and extrinsic motivation. The former addresses a situation in which the child's motivation is internal: he or she engages in homework and studying because he or she is interested, curious, or enjoys learning new things.

Extrinsic motivation, on the other hand, is based on motivational levers that are not personal but are rather due to external factors. Examples are the feeling of satisfaction or the reward obtained from the teacher or parents after getting a good grade. Although the latter is easier to manipulate than the former, intrinsic motivation is a much more powerful engine since it acts directly on the subject. The ways to increase it are different and we will see them later in this chapter.

From apathy to interest

Apathy is always a cause for concern, whether the person is an adult, an adolescent, or a child. This concern is greatest when the individual has difficulty maintaining concentration or learning. Apathy and low interest, in fact, can have a huge influence on one's course of study, career, and activities of everyday life.

Some parents, to combat apathy, become nagging and insist on rereading over and over, making comparisons with other classmates, reiterating concepts again and again, or complaining about the situation. This behavior only increases the distance between the child and parents, increasing disinterest and apathy.

Apathy usually characterizes older children approaching adolescence. This is a time full of major changes, which can create unbalanced situations in children. Another factor that promotes apathy is being placed in a low or over-stimulating environment in which they cannot find or identify something suitable for them. Low self-esteem also plays an important role in apathy: children who feel unappreciated and insecure fail to have a full awareness of their abilities and potential; they prefer not to undertake any activity because they believe they are unable to complete it.

With this in mind, it is important to work first on gaining greater self-confidence, on the one hand by valuing and focusing on the child's strengths and on the other hand by working on what the child feels are his or her weaknesses. In this process, communication between the parents and the child is the key tool as the child must feel free to express himself and externalize his positive and negative emotions.

As far as learning is concerned, the turning point is in identifying the most suitable study method for the child. Turning the time of study and homework into a fun activity will increase both interest and involvement. For example, you can create quizzes, memory cards or other games that will stimulate the child and get him or her excited about the subject.

Tips for increasing motivation in children

As we have learned, motivation is closely related to our perception of ourselves and our ability to achieve one or more goals. For this reason it is important to work on self-esteem and self-awareness. In addition to this there are some tips that can be put into practice to help children develop motivation especially in school.

√ School is not just about studying.

This is where children spend most of their days. It is the place where they meet their friends and form their first social relationships with their peers. It is the facility where they learn to relate to the adult world and face their first problems away from the family unit.

These are important concepts but are often ignored by young children. Teaching them to observe school and everything that happens within it in a different light can be helpful in motivating them to do better or engage in both curricular and extracurricular activities.

√ Agreeing on goals

In order to hold young children accountable and motivate them, it is particularly useful to make charts or blackboards on which to jot down an outcome that the child must achieve. This can be the performance of an exercise, sitting for at least an hour or learning a poem by heart.

What is important is that these goals are decided together with the child, thus giving the child a chance to express his or her opinion and point of view. Upon achievement agree on a small prize or reward that will make him feel gratified: a candy, a night at the movies, an afternoon at the park, and so on.

✓ Using empathy

One of the reasons why children lose motivation, and somehow part of low self-esteem, is not feeling understood or valued. For this reason, it is absolutely essential to avoid denigrating or minimizing the child's activity or achievement.

All efforts, even those that seem the most trivial, for young children require great commitment and willpower. In contrast, empathetic phrases that are able to express closeness, understanding, and satisfaction are effective tools for rekindling motivation in even the most listless and apathetic children.

✓ Exercise.

Although it may seem trivial, exercise is an effective means of reactivating motivation and energy in young and old alike.

Many children now spend much of their days at home playing on computers, tablets, phones or other devices that do not stimulate any kind of physical activity. Lack of exercise, in addition to slowing mental function and motivation, has negative effects on children's overall health.

Chapter 6

—

Advice for parents

Managing emotions as a parent

Many parents of children with diagnosed attention deficit disorder or simple difficulty in concentrating feel guilty, useless and demoralized.

These are emotions that it is normal to feel, especially if one has no experience with these types of situations. Nevertheless, it is crucial to deal with these emotions in a healthy way so as to avoid any negative repercussions in daily life or family relationships.

The most common feeling is guilt; in a sense, parents feel responsible for their child's difficulties. Yet this is not the case. It is a distorted perception that stems from the human need to identify a responsible party to everything bad that happens. Unfortunately, in some cases, it is not possible to pinpoint the cause, all the more so in the case of attention deficit for which, to date, no definite causes have yet been identified that can cause the onset of this type of disorder.

Just as with younger children, Mindfulness is also a very effective practice in adults. Carving out a moment during the day to become aware of the outside world, emotions and feelings can be very helpful in processing anxiety and frustration in a healthy way. In case the situation is more serious, it is advisable to seek the help of a specialist who can provide the necessary tools to overcome the difficulties as best as possible.

In addition, it is important to keep in mind that ADD is not a disabling disease. On the contrary, the sooner it is recognized the sooner it is possible to implement the necessary modifications to support the child's development. For this reason, taking action is a good thing in itself since you are already working to improve the child's life and learning.

Another aspect that is often overlooked by parents is that the attention deficit can also be observed from another point of view: the positive one. True, the child has some difficulty in staying focused and attentive, yet these negative behavioral traits are accompanied by the other side of the coin. For example, a child characterized by impulsive behavior is full of creative energy, while one who is moody and irritable usually is also sensitive and compassionate. Children who tend to be easily distracted are also driven by a lively curiosity about the world around them; those who are hyperactive have the energy for continual adventures and experiences. The more stubborn, on the other hand, are equipped with the determination needed to get their way. Finally, intrusive children are also often enthusiastic and assertive.

Useful tips

The focus of this book is on children with poor attention, yet it is important to devote a moment to parents as well. Children require a lot of energy, especially when they need support to overcome difficulties, but on the other hand it is important for a parent not to forget to also take care of themselves and pay attention to their emotions as well. As mentioned in the previous paragraph, it is normal to feel frustrated or overwhelmed from time to time, which is precisely why it is essential to learn about oneself and recognize the signs of failure. Below are some useful suggestions so that parents can maintain their well-being:

- Take breaks

When you realize you are close to your limit take a break, a kind of time-out to relieve stress and tension.

Especially in cases of children with ADHD, it is normal to feel guilty, frustrated or anxious. Yet you do not have to let this control every aspect of your life: take time to step back from the situation and regain your balance. Only once you have calmed down will you be able to think more clearly and lucidly, thus finding the best way to deal with the situation.

- Try meditation

Meditation is an effective tool for combating stress and anxiety. In general, all practices that focus on deep breathing and relaxation techniques are really helpful in regaining control of emotions. One aspect that some adults tend to underestimate is that the child is observing the parents, so he or she can realize that adults can also feel stressed and learn from them how to calm themselves in certain situations.

Together with the child you can also decide on a code word that you will use whenever you feel overwhelmed or close to your limits. Using that word will allow you to pause the discussion and take a few minutes to breathe and calm down before continuing the discussion in a more balanced and clear-headed way.

- Ask for help if necessary

Don't be afraid to ask for help and support when you need it. Wanting time for yourself is natural and you should not feel guilty about it. You can ask for help from family members or a babysitter and give yourself a chance to unwind, think about yourself and recharge. Do any activity that helps you feel calmer and happier: a walk, go to the gym, read a book, have a relaxing massage, have dinner with friends, go to the movies, and so on.

- Turn to specialists

Professionals who specialize in children with attention deficit disorder can also provide excellent advice to parents. They have a great deal of experience and can therefore give you directions, techniques or exercises to repeat at home to calm you and your child.

Remember that a physically and mentally healthy parent is essential for every child. When you take care of yourself you are also taking care of your child.

Coping with attention deficit in the family

If the child is still very young he may not really understand what is going on. He is full of energy and vitality and sometimes may feel uncomfortable when faced with an activity that requires concentration.

In short, explaining attention deficit to a child is quite complicated and that is also why it should not be the priority. It is best to start the discussion by talking about the situation and the child's emotions, helping them to feel safe and free to confide. Obviously the more they will be able to understand the disorder the better, but it is crucial not to have expectations given their young age.

The message that needs to be conveyed is that the attention deficit they have is not negative, it is merely something that makes them more energetic and dreamy. It is a personality trait like that of other children who are more introverted or shy instead.

Honest and sincere communication must be maintained, guiding the child through the different stages of growth.

The central point is that the child must be able to understand who he is, accepting and appreciating himself in all his facets. It is of primary importance that he does not grow up feeling different in a negative sense. The more positivity a parent is able to instill in his or her child, the greater the likelihood that that child will become an adult capable of managing his or her emotions and achieving the same academic and professional results as his or her peers.

Turning to a more general discussion related to the whole family, a premise must be made: every family unit is different, as is the context. There is no magic recipe capable of making the task of parenting easier as there are thousands of different variables, situations, and personalities.

Nevertheless, the following are tips and reminders that can be helpful to families in which one or more members suffer from attention deficit disorder.

- It's not laziness

Children with attention deficit disorder are not lazy; they are simply choosing the easiest path for them. If your child is hyperactive and cannot sit still in his chair, he is not doing it on purpose or with the intent to annoy you. He is behaving this way because it is really difficult for him to remain still.

- Impulsiveness

If the child is particularly impulsive this behavior stems from an inability to control. Remember that he will tend to act without thought or consequences.

- School Difficulties.

Difficulties in school do not stem from lack of effort or laziness but rather from the fact that concentrating is very difficult for him compared to other children. He should not be blamed for this.

If you notice recurring difficulties, look for alternatives or different approaches that can boost attention. Contact teachers to consider creating ad hoc materials or bringing in support figures who can support the child as he or she learns.

- Inform the whole family

It is essential that all family members know the child's condition and know how to behave in his or her presence. Being aligned is a key element in the child's healthy and positive growth.

Make sure that all adults fully understand the importance of adopting certain behavior and techniques.

- Don't feel alone

Remember that you are not alone and that attention disorders are extremely common. There are support groups and associations that can help families who need help or suggestions on techniques and behaviors to raise their child in the healthiest way possible.

Chapter 7

A practical approach to attention deficit

General Guidelines

Before we delve into the more practical aspect of educational strategies, it is important to remember what guidelines to keep in mind when dealing with a child with poor attention. These are simple instructions that can be applied to almost any aspect of life and can make a real difference in the child's development and relationship with adults.

- Use clear and simple instructions

Often the instructions given by parents are not really clear to children. This argument is even more true in young children with attention deficit disorder.

The best way to educate them is by giving well-structured instructions that cannot be misunderstood: they should be unambiguous and concise so that the child can remember them easily.

If possible, the rules should be few, clear and simple. In addition, it is essential that they be decided together with the child and not against him. Involving him in the process of creating and setting the rules is the best way to make him feel part of the group and push him to follow the rules he has agreed upon.

- Recognizing the child's commitment

By this point in the book, we should have realized that children with AD face many more difficulties in everyday life than their peers. For this reason, it is essential to ensure that they perceive your support without it becoming misplaced or excessive. Affirmations, compliments or acknowledgements that recognize the child's effort and make him or her feel gratified are sufficient. If the outcome is important or extremely positive, there is nothing to prevent rewarding the child with something he or she has wanted for a long time such as a game, outing or activity.

Particular attention should be paid to the use of words and phrases as it is good to avoid generic and impersonal compliments such as "nice job," "wow, that's good" or "congratulations." Choose phrases that are more specific and can highlight the child's work and commitment to that specific activity, for example, "wow, I'm glad you were able to finish the exercises on your own and with the right attitude," or "wow, you tidied up your room impeccably and in the time we agreed on. I'm really happy with how you tackled this task!" In this way convey to the child your interest in his behavior and actions.

- Being positive

Parents should always approach every situation with a positive attitude; even negative circumstances can be viewed from an encouraging perspective. And children with attention deficit need such encouragement even when it comes to small activities or challenges.

In fact, positivity allows for increased confidence and self-esteem in children. The only caution is not to go overboard in pressuring toddlers to be positive all the time; it is normal to have bad moments. Yet, even in those negative moments, the parent must make the child understand that there is nothing wrong with having negative behaviors sometimes.

- Be flexible

There is no question that a child with difficulty in concentrating needs rules, structure and routines; they are essential for development and achievement. Nevertheless, the role of flexibility should not be underestimated.

One must be open to change even when it is sudden or unwanted. Not all rules or routines, in fact, will always be followed perfectly or without contingencies. Flexibility allows one to deal with these situations more lucidly and calmly.

No one person is perfect, no parent or child is. Therefore, we cannot expect perfection from ourselves or our children. Remembering this is enough to relieve stress and allow ourselves some flexibility.

- Determine what is really important

This advice actually applies to all parents. All of us have been children and perhaps some still remember the energy and vitality of those years.

Only once we became parents did we really understand the words and difficulties that faced our mother and father. The challenges a parent faces are so many every day, yet we are human beings and cannot have the energy to fight them all. This is the reason why it is so important to choose the battles worth fighting for.

There is nothing wrong with ignoring the little things sometimes, just as there is nothing wrong with letting the child choose even when he or she does not opt for the best alternative. For example, if the child refuses to eat dinner, do not be afraid to let him skip a meal. If he is hungry before bedtime it will be too late. He has made his choice. Not eating for dinner will not harm him in any way; if anything, he will understand the importance of eating at the appointed dinner time.

- Dividing complex problems into simple tasks
We have already mentioned this point in previous chapters but it deserves to be emphasized again given its importance, especially in children with attention deficits.

Remember that the best way to keep concentration and interest alive is by dividing tasks into simple, easy-to-understand activities. This method allows the child to follow the list step by step, avoiding misunderstandings or forgetfulness. This is a technique that is really effective in people with attention deficit disorder and can be applied throughout their lives.

- Organize your day

Lack of organization can slow down a child's progress as they will tend to get distracted easily and forget things. In this regard, it is important that he or she grows up in an organized space in a way that enhances his or her skills and abilities. This applies to both physical environments such as the house and his room, as well as mental space.

Creating a daily plan with a list of activities and things to do is one of the most effective tools for instilling organization into your child's everyday life. The plan should be drawn up as simply as possible and should contain all the activities and routines that need to be internalized by the child: the morning routine, the routine at school, the homework routine, the routine of time in front of the PC or video games, the routine before bedtime, and so on.

Remember that consistency is a really powerful weapon in children with attention deficit disorder.

- Communicating with the child

Parent-child communication has always been one of the most important tools of family life as it is the best way to educate children.

Knowing how to communicate with your children is essential to becoming better parents and understanding children's thoughts and motivations. Things that seem incomprehensible to us can suddenly become clear when we communicate with the other person.

The goal of every parent should be to create a relationship based on transparent and sincere communication, where each party can feel free to express their emotions and thoughts freely. Many different strategies can be used to do this, for example, one can ask the child to become an active listener and repeat what is said before adding his or her response. Another way is to encourage children to ask questions or seek clarification when they do not understand something, so as to avoid misunderstandings or wrong conclusions.

Finally, positive communication can be emphasized through the elimination of criticism by inviting family members to say nothing when they have nothing nice to say or to add a positive comment before a negative one. In this way, the child will have to make an appreciation first and then say what he or she does not like.

Things not to do

In addition to the general guidelines that it is good to follow to support the child, there are some other things that are good to avoid. These are behaviors and actions that could worsen the child's state of mind and affect the child's attitude and improvement.

X Do not show excessive frustration.

As is well known, parents must have a lot of patience when educating their children, yet it is not easy to maintain it all the time. There are circumstances in which one may go so far as to lose control and be driven by negative emotions, thus showing frustration, anxiety, stress or anger.

The manifestation of these feelings can have negative repercussions on the child: on the one hand, he will feel responsible for your mood, and on the other hand, he will learn to interpret as normal the externalization of aggressive behavior with the risk that he himself will implement the same behavior in social settings.

Instead of getting carried away by anger or stress, it is best to explain as calmly as possible why you are feeling a certain way. By doing so you will talk about your negative emotions openly but without getting carried away by them, and you will teach the child to do the same. Remember that it is yes important for the child to see you even in times of discouragement and difficulty, but it is even more important for him to see the way you react to those situations.

X Avoid negative words and phrases.

Negative words are part of everyday language; they are so ingrained in the way we communicate that we often don't even realize it. Therefore, especially at the beginning, it can be complicated to prevent or recognize the use of negative words at the intent of a sentence or conversation. Some fairly common examples are phrases such as "don't cry," "don't do that," "I don't have time," "I'll help you, you can't," "it's nothing," "stop it or we'll go home," etc.

These are all phrases that have a highly negative effect as they tend to minimize, belittle or limit the child's feelings and emotions. All these phrases can be replaced with positive communication in which, instead of highlighting the negative aspects, the parent approaches the situation in a positive way. As an example, the phrase "I'll help you, you can't" can be replaced with "it sounds like a difficult job, I'll be here by your side and I'll be ready to help you when you need it."

✗ Don't yell

More and more experts are pointing out that yelling is one of the worst educational methods as this attitude only leads to loosening up the child and creating trauma that also affects his or her future adult life.

These considerations are even more important when talking about a child with attention deficit who may already feel insecure or different from his friends. In these cases, shouting only increases his insecurity and the feeling that he is not up to the various situations in front of him.

Once again, positive communication is the key to creating a healthy relationship with children that encourages the development of their potential in a free and open manner.

Creating a routine

Since creating a routine is important in the growth of a child with attention deficit, in this section we will give a practical example using a routine that is necessary for every parent: the one before bedtime. Actually, the steps mentioned can be applied in creating any other routine.

In the specifics of this routine, it is first important to decide on the bedtime and the time to devote to pre-bedtime activities. So that the child arrives at bedtime sufficiently tired, it is recommended that his or her day has included physical activity or outdoor play. Also, it would be best to avoid sweet or sugary snacks.

In general, the steps to follow in creating a routine are as follows:

1. Constancy

It is important to repeat the activities in the routine every day, at the same time and for the same length of time.

In the case of the pre-sleep routine you can remove television, phone or tablet displays at least an hour before, this will help the child understand that bedtime is approaching.

2. Establish a positive association

If possible, you should establish a positive association with the routine you want to establish. Something that will allow the child to build a positive bond and, as a result, entice him or her to stick to it. This can be a game, reading a book, or a special activity dedicated exclusively to bedtime.

3. Include an adjustment period

To prepare the child for routine time, it can be helpful to include a transition time, so the child will understand what is happening. For example, in the case of pre-sleep time, you can devote the 20-30 minutes before to listening to soothing music by dimming the lights.

4. Create a supportive environment

Depending on the routine you want to teach the child, you can modify or adapt the surroundings. You can put into practice small arrangements that are useful in facilitating the child's task by including objects that in a way can guide the child in carrying out the routine. In the pre-sleep routine it may consist of closing the blinds, turning on the fan in the summer, turning on the bedtime lamp, or listening to soothing sounds for sleep conciliation.

Setting the rules

We have already talked about the importance of creating simple and unambiguous rules that children can follow without too much difficulty. This is a key element in the healthy growth of young children, so rules must be decided responsibly and in cooperation with the children. First of all, a distinction must be made between consequences and punishments.

It is now well known that punishments are an ineffective method of discipline since they are based on reprimands, complaints, negative words, deprivation, and physical and verbal violence. Given their nature, they create a negative relationship between parents and children and from which children are unlikely to learn positive and useful values to develop their potential.

Consequences, on the contrary, are based on empowering young children. The core of this approach is to talk openly with children, explaining to them what are the natural consequences of their actions or of not following the rules. This gives children the opportunity to become more aware of their actions and what they may entail.

Below is a series of possible rules that can be established with your children and from which you can determine the consequences if they are not followed.

- Turn off electronic devices 30 minutes before bedtime. This is especially helpful to start the pre-bedtime routine and to encourage reading.

- Do not use your phone during meals. Breakfast, lunch and dinner are three perfect times to strengthen family bonds without the distraction of electronic devices.

- Limit time in front of pc, YouTube or on the phone. If possible, it is best to set up a family environment with few electronic devices so that the child is spurred to play outside, read or use real games. The more children get used to being in front of a screen, the harder it will be to remove this habit.

- Complete the list of the day or routines. It is essential to make sure that the child correctly performs the daily activities or routines that have been agreed upon. Parents should always check that everything has been completed, so as to reward the child if successful or illustrate the consequences if not.

- Finish homework by a set time. Deciding together on the time to devote to homework and study is a good strategy to hold the child accountable and ensure that he or she completes the activity by the set time.

Chapter 8

—

Games and activities to improve attention in toddlers

Concentration games

Board games geared toward the development of concentration are ideal for children with attention deficit disorder.

This type of games is able to stimulate the attention and mental concentration of young children without them experiencing it as an effort or a boring activity. Nowadays there are numerous games on the market geared toward the development of concentration, many of them divided according to the age group of the child.

- Shanghai (5 years and up)
This is a fairly simple game in which each player must try to collect as many sticks as possible without moving everyone else. This game is useful for stimulating sustained attention and logic as the child must stay focused and carefully plan his moves.

- Jenga (ages 6 and up)

Jenga is a game very similar to Shanghai but in this case, instead of sticks, you have bricks that make up a tower. The goal of the game is to be able to remove as many bricks as possible without collapsing the tower.

Jenga is perfect for stimulating sustained attention, logic and planning. It is also especially loved by children who enjoy trying not to collapse the tower and all the bricks in it.

- Cluedo (ages 7 and up)

A great classic that proves effective even for children with attention deficits. This board game requires a lot of attention and logic as you need to collect the clues needed to find out who the murderer is.

- Uno (ages 8 and up)

Uno is the perfect card game to stimulate sustained attention and logic. The object of the game is to run out of cards by creating color and number matches or by taking advantage of special cards.

- Find the differences

This type of game can stimulate concentration and the use of a systematic method for analysis and observation. The goal is to identify the differences between two images that, at first glance, appear identical. There are games of this type suitable for all ages.

Strategy Games

Games based on reasoning and strategy can be excellent allies for developing concentration and analytical thinking. In fact, strategy and attention are closely linked since there can be no programming without an appropriate level of concentration.

It is essential for the child to develop the ability to reason and strategy; it is a useful skill in every area of life: school, work, family and relationships.

- Legos (ages 2 and up)

Legos among the first and most beloved toys in most children's lives. The best thing about the famous building sticks is that they are useful for developing strategy and planning in children of all ages.

- Tangram (ages 5 and up)

Tangram can develop attention, logic and strategy. In this board game, the child must be able to reproduce different figures such as animals, boats or rockets using 7 wooden tablets. In this process, the child is stimulated to reason in order to succeed in getting the figure he or she wants.

- Force 4 (ages 6 and up)

Another great board game classic, Forza 4 has the ability to increase concentration and strategy in a simple and fun way.

The aim of the game in this case is twofold: on the one hand to line up the 4 tokens of one's own color, and on the other hand to prevent the other player from succeeding first. Having a dual goal provides the perfect stimulus for children with attention deficits.

- Checkers (ages 7/8 and up)

In older children, Checkers may be the most suitable solution. Although the rules of the game are simple, it is a game that requires a lot of concentration and good skills in planning and choosing a strategy that leads to victory.

Memory Games

Memory is a quality that is often lacking in children with attention difficulties. Constant distractions, in fact, prevent the assimilation of information and to limit the amount of information that is remembered.

Memory is important to a child's schooling, learning, and personal life, so it is advisable to focus on developing this skill from as early as possible.

- Memory (ages 3 and up)

Memory involves recognizing matching pairs of cards within a deck. There are different versions of this that are adapted to the different ages of the child and can therefore be more or less complicated.

This game on the one hand develops memory and on the other sustained and selective attention in order to remember which cards have been discovered and their position.

- Guess Who (ages 6 and up)
Another great classic among board games. The strength of Guess Who lies in the fact that the child is stimulated to listen and remember which questions have already been asked in order to be able to select the characters that have the correct characteristics.

- Chess (ages 7/8 and up)
For children with attention deficit, the game of Chess is an excellent strategy for enhancing attention span, strategy and memory. By striving to remember the rules of the game and the movements each piece can make, the child develops the memory and logic needed to win.

Sport

Sports and physical activity more generally are two key factors in the management of children with attention deficit disorder. Indeed, studies have shown that there are sports activities that can reduce symptoms related to poor attention, hyperactivity, and impulsivity.

In addition, physical activity in social settings promotes self-control, social and interpersonal skills, cooperation, respect for rules, and stress management.

- Swimming

This sport is among the most recommended sports for children with AD who appreciate structured sports. Although it is a single sport, it is practiced in an environment full of peers and instructors, stimulating the child's social skills.

- Martial Arts

Martial arts can prove to be a truly powerful tool. In fact, this sport is based on self-control, respect and discipline, all of which can provide valuable support for the development of a child's potential. There are also two other advantages: on the one hand, the practice is full of rituals that are useful in instilling the concept of routine, while on the other hand, the child must carry out the instructor's instructions step by step, thus limiting the possibility of distraction.

- Tennis

This sport is suitable for children who enjoy competition. The strength of tennis lies in the fact that it is characterized by a fast pace that helps to keep concentration. The gesture and physical exertion required can also be helpful in releasing the child from any stress or tension accumulated during the day.

- Soccer/volleyball

These types of sports are especially suitable for children who need to develop social and interpersonal skills. They are the ultimate group sports and are based on achieving a common goal: working together to win the game. This "teamwork" can be helpful in developing self-esteem and awareness in the child.

Creative activities

Many creative activities are used by experts to help children develop different psychological and brain areas while having fun. They also provide a channel through which toddlers can channel their emotions in a positive way.

There are so many creative activities, in this paragraph we will look at just a few of the endless options available.

- Painting with watercolors (ages 2 and up)

As soon as the child is able to recognize and appreciate colors, it is possible to introduce him or her to the world of painting and drawing. Drawing and coloring are two useful activities for developing concentration and creativity, and can keep even the most lively and impulsive temperaments in check.

- Fantasy games (ages 3 and up)

This category includes all games in which the child pretends to be a character and initiates a story or skit. This type of activity is recommended for children characterized by an explosive personality and with difficulties in channeling their emotions.

In fact, through the invention of stories, children can freely express their emotions.

These include playing with dolls, a doctor's kit or puppets.

- Playing a musical instrument (ages 5 and up)

Music engages both hemispheres of the brain, thus strengthening the ability to multi-task at the same time. It is a fun and stimulating activity that educates children to concentrate, listen and respect rules and timing.

- Cooking (ages 5 and up)

Many children enjoy helping adults in the kitchen and making cookies, cakes or other simple dishes. Time spent among the stove not only makes their tummies happy but also leaves a positive mark on their personalities.

The kitchen is an environment that requires concentration and attention, especially when you have to follow the instructions and steps provided by adults.

- Theater (ages 6 and up)

Children who enjoy acting, being the center of attention, and communicating to an audience may enjoy theater activities.

Deciding to participate in a play is an important step in a child's growth as it requires commitment, dedication, memory development to learn the part, and the ability to relate to the group. Finally, the applause of the audience at the end is the icing on the cake that is useful in boosting the child's self-esteem.

Conclusion

Raising a child who has difficulty focusing and maintaining attention can be exhausting, but nothing surpasses the wonderful times spent together. What is important is to be aware that adversity and difficulties are part of every parent's journey; the difference lies in how you decide to deal with them.

Reading this book has already provided you with useful tools to support your child in growing and developing his or her potential. Do not be afraid to experiment, try, fail and start again. Attempt until you find the activities, routines and rules that best suit your child. Above all, remember to always communicate openly and calmly. Communication is the cornerstone of the relationship with toddlers and is the key through which we can enter into their feelings and emotions. Only by discovering their inner world, in fact, can we help them in expressing themselves freely in the outside world as well.

Do not underestimate the importance of thinking about yourself either, taking a break or asking for help when needed. Abandon guilt because thinking about your own well-being means thinking about the well-being of your child as well, who needs a balanced and calm parent.

Attention deficit does not have to be a limitation. As we have learned in this book there are plenty of tools that family, teachers, and friends can implement to overcome this small obstacle. All that remains is to get started!

Printed in Dunstable, United Kingdom